Fastest Way To Recruit A-Players

MIKE AGUGLIARO

ISBN-13: 978-1541063464
ISBN-10: 1541063465

CEOWARRIOR.com

BOOM!

Boom!

Hey, it's Mike Agugliaro, Business Warrior -- with some insight to share that's real, raw, relevant, and right now!

You've opened this report and started reading. Congratulations – this one seemingly simple step now puts you head-and-shoulders above many other business owners whose businesses are stuck in the "I-wish-it-was-different" spiral of death.

But you took the first step to get your hands on this book, and the second step to open it and read it.

Now the third step is something you may not have thought about yet – *how will you apply what you read?*

Some people will skim this report and put it on a shelf. Six months from now they'll wonder why it didn't help them.

However, I don't want to waste your time and I don't want you to waste mine, so I have a challenge for you. It's something I personally do daily and it helped to change the game for me.

Rather than reading (skimming) and putting the book away, I advise that you read actively, with a pen and highlighter in hand, and a notepad and some sticky notes nearby.

Underline and star important points; jot down notes as you go. Add sticky notes of points to revisit later. Later in this report is a TAKE ACTION section that gives you space for specific types of actions (I use a page like that whenever I read anything.)

If you've never read a book this way before, you might feel strange writing in it but I promise you: it will completely change how you read, and how much you'll benefit from what you read. (I devour books this way and the notes are beneficial to me when I re-read and review books again and again.)

I want you to enjoy a massive amount of wealth, freedom, and market domination (however you choose to define those terms in your life and business)… and actively reading this report will help you unlock more of those things for you.

What I share in this report are strategies/ideas/concepts/tools that I still use daily in my $30+ million/year business. I know these work in my business and I share them with you so you can apply them in yours too. (These are exactly the same kinds of strategies I share in my 4-day Warrior Fast Track Academy.)

By the way, I always want to serve you at the highest level, so make sure you read all the way through to the end of the book because I have some bonus material and resources in the back that I think you'll love.

Ready? Let's dig in and get you more wealth, freedom, and market domination right now...

This document is an edited transcription from a presentation Mike delivered. Some of the content has been edited for clarity, while some content retains its verbal style.

FASTEST WAY TO RECRUIT A-PLAYERS

I'm going to give it to you as real and raw as I can give it. I'm going to share as much as I can so there's going to be no tricks. I'm pulling no punches. We're going to throw it out there and I'm going to share everything. I see I have lots of friends on the phone. I see I got some clients on the phone. How do I know? Your name comes up on my cool little instant teleseminar thing. Which, by the way, 1 thing you might as well know about me, whatever comes to my mind I'm going to let it come out my mouth even if you don't like it.

My wife says I should not let everything that comes in my mind out my mouth, but today she's not in the room and I'm doing this call from my dojo, my martial arts studio in my house. I'm running on jet fuel today because I've learned when you have a level of endurance, with endurance enough energy in your physical body and mind and your spirit that you can just drive massive, massive results.

One thing I'll tell you if any of you guys got crews all over and you're still dragging them in every morning from their family to give them a coaching session, I have no idea why you would not use a device like this instant teleseminar and tell them to call in the morning so they can sit in their underwear, eat their breakfast with their family, love and hug their wife, and I could coach them for 5, 10, 15 minutes in a huddle. I have no idea why I'd need them to come to the shop to do that. I could train them, coach them, and manage them, right?

That's not what today's about. Today is about recruiting and we will jump into that. Every time I see a nugget like this I want to let you think a little different, hear things a little different than you may have ever heard it before. That's what we're going to do.

I'm Mike Agugliaro, you probably figured that out by now, again I'm so happy that you're looking ... I'll control the noise on this side. I'm so glad you're on the phone because it means, you know what, you care enough, or you're desperate enough, or you just want more for your business and life and that's why you're looking to see how you can get more A players. I'll break some of the mysteries down and some of the myths and probably a whole bunch of stuff that other gurus and everybody else is telling you.

My stuff might sound a little bit different, but that's okay, right? We did 23.5 million last year. We have 145 employees. 100 trucks to the fleet, and if you haven't figured this out, this is going to come fast and furious today, right. That's how we're going to deliver this. Don't worry if you don't hear all the information because I'm probably programming it into your mind to have you run at the highest level performance human being that you can.

This is all about you, right, this is about serving you and serving what I believe has given me one of the most amazing lives on the planet today. It has delivered massive wealth for me, tons of freedom, demanded a lot of market domination, and I'm very passionate about trades people. Being an electrician and only being about 11 years it's only 11 years ago roughly, a little less, I was still climbing in attics and digging ditches with a pick ax. I just told the guys today don't ever challenge me to go back out there. I don't want to go back out there, but if I do have the level of endurance and mindset I will climb through an attic, pull wire, or bending PVC I will do whatever it takes today.

I can relate to you guys and I also believe success leaves clues, right? If you're struggling it's not a market, it's not an environment, it's not a people thing, it's probably not even a you thing, it just means you need to figure some things out, right? We need to just do things a little different.

If you haven't read the book, *Who Moved My Cheese*, you might as well read it and read it again and read it again. It is the number 1 thing I reminded myself going into the economy that has hurt most people, it's the number 1 thing I reminded myself. I ask myself every day, is the cheese moving and where is it moving? You want to make sure you're writing these cheese statements down. Every now and then I'll give you a little pause to take a sip of water, relax your brain, let it expand, and then kind of come back to normal.

You want to ask yourself, where is the cheese moving? That's why I've never in the last 10 years had a down year or flat year and I've always made an extra billion a year. That's the bottom line. That's how we did 23.5 million. Now I'm not going to pull that stuff and go out there like some people today where they're like, I made 23 million, yeah, it was like 2 million a year for like over 10 years, right. That's just crazy. I'm talking 23.5 million last year and we cranked over whatever it was 18% profit. That's how we ended off last year. I was happy as a pig in crap, right.

That's why I want to just tell you guys what we're delivering. Pay attention to it. Ask yourself, where is the cheese moving? I know the cheese has moved because the way you used to hire people before is different now. The people are different. Their minds are different. The generation is different. We'll get into all that stuff; so I don't forget, I got tons like, look, I don't want to be your guru. I want to be a supporter to you guys. I don't want you, I'm not the guy you want to put in front of your company. Anytime you put a guru in front of your company he all of a sudden will inject something into your culture and maybe it's not 100% fit.

What I do want to do is I want to be a behind-the-scenes, for you, mentor, right. I want to tell you things no one else is telling you so you can take action. Please, if you do anything of mine that takes action go out there and just tell people I'm cool and a rock star and a ninja and I'll love you for that. My podcast is out there. Jump on that thing, I'm interviewing all kinds of amazing people. You can go to secrets of business mastery podcast. I'm a publisher of a magazine, *Home ServiceMAX* mag. We got guys like Mike Michalowicz in there and Karyn Greenstreet. It's off the hook.

I built the podcast to interview people I wanted to learn from so I could deliver to guys like you and ladies like you today. Home Service Max mag I took on to be a publisher of that magazine because I wanted to deliver content, the real deal that I always wanted. Plus, just jump on all my social media stuff, Facebook and most of you guys that I see on the call are following me anyways.

What are we going to learn today, right? Today is learn how to create and train A players for the fastest and easiest way possible to build a team that will grow your business. Here's the thing that maybe some of you know and some don't know: I have an amazing team. We have 145 employees now. I don't have an office in my building for the last 3 years now. There's only 2 partners there, it's me and Rob. I can relate to everything that any one of you will tell me.

You want to tell me about bad partnerships? That's cool. I know all about it. You want to tell me about a brand new truck 2 weeks old sprinter, flips over, catches fire, and has to be thrown out? I got it. You want to talk to me about 5 employees leaving all in the same week to start their own business? I got it. You want to talk about general managers and people that'll rip you off and take advantage of you and make you feel like they've stabbed you in the back 100 times? I can talk about it.

I want you to know the reason you're on this call today is not about hiring and training A players, it's because you're pretty sure I know something right now, not because I'm not going to try to impress any of you, just impress upon you strategies that you can use, right? I want you to solve your problems. One thing I'll just get out right now, like look, if you're all about me, you're one of those people in the world that's all about I. You care nothing but just about yourself. This information is a waste because this information is made to serve great people who want to serve their employees. They want to serve their company, they want to serve their customer. Yes, they want to serve their vendors and their family at the very high end level possible.

Make sure you've got something to take notes on. Some of you guys may be recording, that's cool too, just don't share it anywhere else because this is for the brave that have jumped on the phone and are dedicating the time to listen to this call. I get it, right, all of you think you're competing against everybody else for employees. We'll talk through that stuff. We're only competing 1 day only against 1 thing. It's us against us. That's all you're doing. You're competing against yourself.

All the results you have are based on the level of exactly how you are, who you are, and what you do as a person. You got crappy results, you're probably doing crappy things. You probably have a crappy attitude. If you're doing amazing things you're probably an amazing person, you're probably doing amazing things, you get amazing results. That's what I've learned.

We'll talk about how to stop the struggling to find the best employee, right, for your service business or whatever you need. Also, we'll hit a little bit on what is recruiting? I always tell people and they're like, "Oh, I can't ... I can never find great people, Mike," and, "It's so hard and there's nobody in my market." I'm like, "Dude, how many people live in your area?" There are like 8 zillion people. I'm like, "So you're telling me out of 8 million people there ain't one good electrician, HVAC tech, plumber, or sewer and drain guy? That's what you're telling me, out of 8 zillion people?" Then that's only in your state? Do you back up to another state that's like 5 minutes over the line?

Is there somebody across the world that would fly here and live here, so blinders on you can't even see how stupid it is what you're saying. I used to love 10 years ago people would always tell me, "Hey, Mike, yeah, right, finding great people, right, everybody." I'm like, "No, don't put me in your crappy ass little bucket of problems that you want." No, I don't understand that. No, I don't get that at all. Yes, I have amazing people. Have I lost some? Yes, I've lost amazing people. Do I get more? Yes, I've gotten more amazing people.

Don't put me in your bracket of limiting beliefs that are serving you not at all and you want to try to give them to try serve me. No, I won't accept them. We'll talk about some of the strategies, the fastest way to recruit these guys, right, and just remember, look, if you're recruiting and getting them in and losing them, well you just got a whole different problem there. We'll address both of those. All right? We'll identify some of the characteristics of a perfect employee, or what we think perfect should be. Then we'll talk about just attracting these A players like a magnet.

Now, I want you to ask some things in your brain. You can answer it out loud, you can answer it on a piece of paper, you can just answer it in your mind if you want. Here's some things you want to think about: 1, are you feeling hostage to your employees you have now on your team? Think about that. If anybody's feeling hostage right now because you have 1, 2, or 1 A player.

Yeah, I get it, right? I felt hostage at one time, too. It was like, oh man, if this manager leaves, or if oh man, if my number 1 person leaves. We'll address some of that because you want to look at the problem before it becomes a problem. Then you want to ask yourself, how much does it cost you to keep bad employees on your team? Yeah, just bleeding you right, those bottom 20%-ers just sucking on the system, right, sucking it dry. You're loyal to them, giving them a job, and they're just bleeding and poking holes in the bucket. All right, cool, we had about 30% of you have that.

How many of you feel like you have a revolving wheel of employees? They come in, they quit, they come in, they quit, they come in, they quit.

I'm going to tell you something else, and I said a little bit in the beginning that I learned, as much as service business owners and entrepreneurs want to be honest, they're so damn liars what they're like. They lie and act like things are good. They don't tell the truth to people. I remember because I used to go in the supply house and I used to be like, "Hey, man, how's work going?" They would go, "Yeah, everything's going great." Then you find out the guy's out of business next week, right. Liar. Liar. Liar.

I remember how many people when I joined an organization, it was over 10 years ago, I would walk around and the 1st thing they'd ask, "How many trucks you got," right? I'd be like, "I got 1. I got 1 truck." They'd be like, "Oh," they'd walk away from me and snub nose me because they had like 20 trucks. Yes, 18 of them were sitting with no insurance on it, because they didn't even know how to figure it out. They were so into their own personal ego they couldn't tell the truth. They were so blind. That's the one thing I've never forgot. I've never forgot where I was 10 years ago.

See, most people have forgotten and they could care less about you. I'm never going to name any names of this company, but you know the big companies out there today that act like they're your friend and then they stomp you in the face, kick you in the throat a little bit. There is no friends. I will tell you, you have a friend right here. I'm going to give you the friend stuff. I want you to do amazing. I don't care if you're in New Jersey or in my backyard.

I want you to do amazing because the more that we ... It used to be like you would join these different things, and I'm not mocking an organization. Organizations are great. I'm just giving you feedback of things that are good and not good. If we all fight as 1 team, universal team, and we raise it to the top we'll all do better. There will be a unified front instead of this brotherhood that you act like there's a unified front and there's no front. That's what I want to do today. Let's show us how to raise the bar.

The other thing is, how much does it cost you to hire bad, like holy crap, right? Spending the time, this energy, give sign-on bonuses, I've never paid out a sign-on bonus. I just want to tell you guys that. I never did it. I never begged anybody to come and work for me ever. I never did it. It'll become apparent why I've never had to beg and I've never had to, like a prostitute, buy love from an employee. You'll know why by the time we're done with this call. Then you can send me a private message and be like, "I get it.

I get it why you're not paying for prostitution and paying for employees." Some of you you're feeling real dirty now. You're like, oh man, I didn't think of it that way when I gave the guy a few thousand dollar sign-on bonus. I thought that was cool. I didn't know I was buying prostitution. I feel so dirty now. Okay, don't worry about feeling dirty. Let's just learn and move forward. Some of you are probably laughing your damn ass off right now over that, and that's cool because it was pretty darn funny. I just actually thought of that just now.

Okay, so here's my big promise to you today, because I believe you need a big promise. I want you to stay on the whole call. We're going to stick to about an hour, but I'm going to tell you right now we're probably going to go about 15 or 20 minutes over. I guarantee the last 20 minutes are probably the best. If you jump off, I'm not sharing this recording with nobody. This is a one-shot deal. If you missed it there ain't no chance. I ain't sharing it with nobody. I'm going to give the love once and to the people who showed up here.

My big promise is that you're going to be able to take items that you can implement tomorrow. You're going to be able to bring this to your team, get focused. You're going to understand how to get A players and create A players. Okay, and this is going to work for any company out there, even if you're a one-man. I'm going to tell you how to get out of kind of that one-man show with a new employees. I don't care if you have more employees than me.

I know a lot of people out there. There's huge companies. I'm friends with a company that's going to do like 160 million. I think he's amazing. Do I think he's better than me? No, I don't. Do I think he craps in the toilet? Yes, he does. He eats just like me. I'm not impressed with anybody and I don't want you to be impressed with me either. I just want you to be impressed with yourself tomorrow when you look in the mirror and know that you're fighting doing the very best you can to change the game. That's what I want.

There might be women on the call and it's cool, but the majority of service business owners are men, decapitated men, right, like they've cut everything off and they're like whimpy-ass humans today. They stop fighting. I want you all to act like, remember the ... Go back when you first started business. Remember how hungry you were? You told everybody about it. The people in the store, and your neighbors, and your friends, and then you get comfortable.

Then you get fat and comfortable and lazy, right? Some of you are like, Mike, I don't know who you're talking to. I'm working my ass off. Yeah, I worked for a boss, wow, it's probably 28 years ago or something. He said, "Mike, it's not that I'm working so much faster than you, I'm just working so much smarter than you."

Some of you guys might have come across this, but you don't know me enough, right. Those who heard my story hear it again for a minute. Just be still, listen to it, we'll get through it fast, but those that never heard of me I want you to know the story. It's only 11 years ago me and my partner, Rob, we're still driving in a van. We were working 6 and 7 days a week. I mean I'm an electrician by trade, we're pulling wires, we were eating insulation, we were digging ditches. As a matter of fact it took me like 8 years before I bought a trencher because I thought it was physical martial arts training for me to go out there and pick ax 20" deep for 200 feet through shale. I thought it was training. That was stupid so we bought a trencher.

It's only 11 years ago I'm in a truck. The wake-up call for me, in case you don't know, for me is that I almost missed the birth of my first child. Then my wife was concerned, she's like, holy mackerel, how was the job today? There was a newborn, we just did the whole crying thing birth, it was the most amazing thing in my life, but she wanted to know how the job went. I mean this was craziness. Some of you guys are still living through this stuff and you're in business 20 years.

You got no more time to figure it out. If you want to see pain, sometimes I ask myself, if I stayed where I was 11 years ago and I just kept going that path, I would be a crippled, burnt out, wrinkly-skinned person like dying. I would have probably been dead, fatigued, burnt out, probably living in the streets because I'd have been so crazy. I understand this stuff, and that was one of the turning points for me.

I want you to know that when you put the right things in place, and I will not tell you it's easy to put the right things in place. You have to turn into a hulk. You have to be strong physically, mentally, and spiritually to grow a company. We already talked you can't be self-serving. That's what I learned. When I put these things in place that's how we went from under a million, okay, and I'm looking at the companies on this call so I know I got 6, 10, and 15 million dollar companies. You guys are doing amazing. I congratulate you, too. I understand that you feel good and you also feel unsatisfied. That's the hunger that breeds.

I've learned that with the stuff that I teach and different things that, and the stuff I'm doing today, that we are changing every day. Every day things are going in place. That's a little bit about my story. Now, I was in the office today and then I came home to do what I call Warrior call with 32 companies I'm working with around the United States, Australia, and Canada, and then I'm doing this call now, which we already talked about what this call's about.

Let's get into the agenda, okay, now you're going to need to write. You're going to need to shorthand this stuff.

The first thing about recruiting A players, you need to identify the needs that you need before you need it. You need to identify the needs you need before you need it. Most of you are trying to solve the problem you have today. You're not forecasting the problem that's going to happen in the future, so you can't get out of the damn kitchen. You need to say to yourself, okay, if I grow this year I'm going to need this next year.

Fastest Way To Recruit A-Players
By Mike Agugliaro

If you need 1 now, you don't need 1, you need 3. Your target has to be 3. Second thing is, you got to know what is missing. What is missing from my team? What do I need to bring in? I have a proven track record, proven track record to bring in people that are just a little bit handy, can use a screw gun, mechanically inclined, make them parts runners, drive parts around, and in 6 months or less turn them into high-performance A players and then take them from high-performance A players and turn them into sales people and managers. Proven system that I've done over and over.

My director, one of the number 1 people below me and Rob started with me as a plumber and HVAC guy, was a sales manager, moved into a couple other positions. Now he's a director. I have this all through my whole company that I've done this with. The reason I did it was I understood what was missing and what was I going to need before I need it, so I wasn't suffering when it was time to get there.

Now I will tell you I never hire per season. I know there's a lot of companies that's their belief. They're like the pool company. They hire for seasons. When the season's over they let them go. I've never done that. I hire, I keep them as family, they come in, I don't want them to leave. I give them overtime when there's lots of overtime. Nobody in my company is ever saying, "I want overtime," and they don't get it. They get more overtime than they want.

The 2nd thing is, or I should say the 3rd thing is what are the results you're not getting? This is all about identify. What are the results you are not getting today? Okay, you're not getting a good enough conversion. You're not getting a good enough average invoice. You're not getting enough revenue. What are the results? You got to answer these questions. We're going through a process right now to identify things and then give strategies to fix them.

Another question is, why don't you have A players? Answer that question out loud to yourself. Why don't you have A players or more A players? We know they're out there. Don't tell me there's not a lot of them. No, there's a reason why they're not with you. That's a fact. There's a reason they're not with you. We'll talk about some of those reasons.

The question you want to ask yourself is, is it you need A players or you're failing to convert B and C players into A players? I will tell you that the majority of the time the problem in businesses today is the leaders and managers are failures to convert B and C players into A players. It's easier to try to hire an A player than change their leadership ability, their training ability, their coaching ability, and their managing ability. I know, and I'm not going to go too deep into it, I know why you can't convert B and C players into A players because you don't understand the first 3 pillars of business: mindset, skillset, and action set.

If you understood how to help train the mind of an employee and help them understand how to shift things that are holding them back, you can easily turn C to B and B to A players. Most of you have not figured that out because you have not been strong enough to convert your own mind to become the leader it takes to convert them.

Again, when you look in the mirror you might need to point the fingers back. Now I'm not telling you this to feel bad. I'm telling you this so you could go, oh snap, you know what, Mike? That made sense to me. I need to figure out how to fix myself and it will fix my company.

I have tons of A players. My goodness, I think I have almost all A players. Those that aren't A players are becoming A players right now because I understand how to go in and set the mindset, the skillset, and the action set. I understand how to create these clarity, the alignment, and the accountability. I understand how to manage, coach, and train and I understand why every one of these are different and my management team and my directors and my team leaders they all understand this philosophy too and how to implement it.

The question is, and I've been following this belief for a long time being a martial arts instructor over 25 years and doing martial arts for over 30 years, I believe there's no bad students, only bad teachers. Now, I understand I can't a lot of times you got a heroin addict he's a heroin addict, don't get all freaky on me and start saying, I don't know your position. I get it. If they have some kind of addiction or something or alcohol, and yeah, mindset will change that, probably not your job to do it. Understand that might be a different story.

I'm talking about the guy that hasn't figured things out. That hasn't learned how to convert or how to serve customers at the highest level. Why don't we ask this? It's not even on my thing here. Why don't we ask ourselves this? Are we a culture of serving customers to make the very best decision for their family or you're still prescribing to all the sales bullshit out there today on sell, sell, sell people, and tell them this ninja? Tell them, throw this in their eyeball and use this magic phrase. Do you ever wonder everybody's still looking for the same magic phrase to use for the same objection instead of just serving the customer through your marketing, through your 1st interaction call, through your pre-rapport formula before you get to the customer's house, then at the customer's house serve them more?

See my dad had no training at all. He had none. There was no training when you go back 50 years ago. They didn't have all that. Yeah, I know Brian Tracy was around a little bit, but not like you have them today. I'm not mocking that you shouldn't get better in your level of communication. I'm just telling you that you have to think about it different. Why are you even on this call today for the A players? I believe you have a company full of A players. I need to fix you and your mindset and your skillset so you can fix them and get them really fast producing the results that serve customers. That's what I believe.

That's it. I'm not giving it to hurt your feelings. I'm giving it because I care about this industry unlike anybody else. Okay, that's why I'm fighting. See I'm not fighting for myself. Before I started this coaching and the books and all the stuff you see me doing. I've already been successful.

My life has already been amazing. I've already got everything. I'm doing this because I will create a movement that changes more lives today than anybody. This outdated bull that everybody's trying to do, these old methods that worked 20 years ago don't work today. People have changed.

All right, so let's talk about you. Will you, and I'm talking about you, attract the people you need? I know how it's easy to be nasty, because look, you're hearing me today 15 years ago and there's very few on this call, but a couple guys know me from the beginning, I don't even like people 15 years ago. I can't even stand people. Everybody aggravated me. See, that's what I was taught, and that's what I attracted. I had every excuse under the sun.

They're going to Rob from me. They're lazy. They're stupid. I said everything. I didn't realize how I was is what I was attracting. I was attracting other nasty people. I was attracting, right, now, I've never been sloppy, but I know sloppy people attract sloppy people. I love when sometimes I see an owner and they're like, "Yeah, my guy's truck is really sad." I look at the owner's car, his car is disgusting. I'm like, no kidding that your guys are disgusting, you're disgusting. Why don't you stop 1st? You're going to attracts that.

The other thing is look, I do believe in universal laws and laws of attraction and all this stuff. Now, I don't believe you can stand in a room and say give me a million, give me a million, and it's going to fall through the sky on your face. I believe that if you don't take a step and change things you're not going to get anything. Here's what I'm going to tell you. If your mindset sucks, and you're doing all those things I did all those years ago, everybody's going to rob from you, they're going to be lazy. I bet if I bring in a guy with a license he's going to do his own business on the side.

I don't believe in any of that and I have tons of people that work with me, had their own licenses, had their own businesses, I don't believe that so I don't attract it. Will it happen? I don't know if it will happen. I don't attract it so I don't believe it ever will. When you turn your mindset into attracting A players you will start to attract the players. When you turn your mindset instead of judging everybody on your team and start serving your employees on the team, now it's what you think they need is what they need.

If you're standing, I love it, my kids are home schooled. My 13-year-old, my son's going to be 16 May 29th. I'll be 45 on May 29th, we share the same birthday, one of the greatest gifts I ever got. He was born 4 weeks early, but here's one thing I always have, and they're home schooled. The public school system is like, "We try to teach all kids." Put them in a square box and try to teach them all the same way. Try to sit in front of a room and show slides to a plumber and an electrician who is kinesthetic in the way they learn is by touching stuff. Holy crap, what are you doing? The guy's never going to learn that way.

You got to know how to deliver the information. You have to be able to make it auditory or kinesthetic, whatever is going to serve them. You have to be able to reframe it. This thought of teaching everybody in your company the same thing at the same time the same way is crippling. I hope that's a big ah-ha for some of you guys, because that's what you're trying to do. Funnel them into a heard, let's try to teach them all the same thing, look, 80/20 rule says 20% of them will figure it out and 80% won't. You have to do things different to get that. You have to share this information so they get it.

If it's all about you and not about them that's what you're going to attract. Also, some of you guys have limiting beliefs. I'm a big limiting-belief guy because I believe limiting beliefs attract and keep you exactly what you have. Limiting beliefs are self-sabotage. Were you ever really, really successful and all of a sudden you become unsuccessful because you have a self-sabotage limiting belief inside your subconscious mind that says when you get close to success and the tipping point you'll sabotage yourself and you'll pull back.

It becomes this cycle. When they say it repeats itself, right, things repeat themselves it's because it does. If you have that self-sabotaging stuff that happens in your brain. I always said to people, most people are always looking at the competition ahead. I'm always just looking behind me. I never worry about what's in front of me. How do you stop a Sherman tank? How do you stop a freight train? It's hard. I don't care if you're a one-person freight train or a 140-person freight train. I'm a freight train. As long as I focus on strategy every day I fight forward every day. I'm going to attract these people and I'm going to get the results.

Number 1, identify what you need and identify to yourself why you may not be getting it. You had to answer all those questions. Number 2 is you got to identify your culture. Ask yourself, if I went to interview for that company, would I work there? Would I work there? I love the people they're in their truck and they got an outline on the door. They're like, "The wrench goes here. The pipe putty goes here. Everything's got it's own little place." I'm like, oh, wow, that's an amazing truck. Does it make any money? I wonder if your guys love you or hate your guts? When it's 9:00 at night, I get a truck should be clean, but there's a thing between clean and fanatically crazy.

You got to ask yourself, who's that serving? Oh, I forgot, you're always worried about being judged by everybody that's going to see your fancy-ass back of your truck. Most of the time that's not making you money. Now I'm not telling you be a slob. I'm telling you guys identify this thing in your culture on how will it look? How will it feel? What is the atmosphere going to be? Some people just need some paint. They're bringing people like look, if your shop and office is in your house, that's the type of employees you're going to attract. They're never going to believe you have the best benefits.

I'm not telling you go rent a room out in the Ritz Carlton. You can have a little room. I was hiring people and we had a little office building, actually it was half martial arts half office. It was a tiny little office, you can see it on my Facebook, and we had a trailer in the back. See I still made sure when they entered the domain of the office that it felt like huge. You got to remember you cannot hire people to come into a company, right, you can't make $20,000,000 with a $10,000,000 mind. You can't make a $5,000,000 business with a $100,000 mind. You can't do it. You can't hire that way either.

Then is the culture a culture of learning and growing or we talked about is it a culture of selling? Selling culture will push people away, will repel them away. A culture of serving will attract them in. We just had what I call a hiring experience, and I know a lot of people have heard this and some have seen it for real time if they come to my 3- or 4-day event. I get in some are like, "Oh, I had hiring fairs." I'm like, "Don't tell me what you had." If you haven't seen what I did, you've never seen anything. You've never seen 50 people in a room begging to work for me and me hire 11 or 15 of them. Yeah, that's just two months ago. Two months ago, right, because anytime you're saying I understand, I got this, Mike, I'm like, do you? Are you answering my questions like you know everything? Jump off the call, otherwise ask yourself, how can I do what I'm doing better? That's what this is about.

What do other employees say about your company? What do they say about your company? See, sometimes you just got to take the hard truth. Survey your employees. Now you should be surveying your employees minimum twice a year, minimum. It could be as simple as, what's going great? What sucks? What would you like us to change? If I was having a problem hiring I would survey not only my employees, I would survey ex-employees and tell them I'll give you $50 to give me the answers. Pay them. Pay them $50 to give you the answer. Why are you not with me now? I want to get better. They'll give you the answer if you open the door for transparent truth.

Sometimes they'll tell you, your benefits suck. Anybody who thinks it's all about pay, I will tell you there's a lot of companies around me that pay more than me. I will tell you those companies that pay more will never fight for their employee's livelihood as I do. They will never have the proven track record as I will. I know that for a fact. Survey your employees, get the hard truth.

You have to look at your culture. Is your culture a thriving culture of always looking for the best team player? Are they always looking for amazing people? In a minute I'm going to answer a question for you guys. Let me answer it now. I know I have it somewhere later down. The question that I hear all the time is, "Mike, well, I don't even have enough work for someone else." I'm like, "Okay, well, when you have work, what will you do?" Here's the magic. First off, so many people know the philosophy you never stop recruiting, but they do stop with the same level of energy of recruiting as when they need somebody.

See, we recruit 100% with 100% of the energy every single day, every day. Me too, every day. I've hired a telemarketer who calls my house. Most of you are hanging up on the telemarketer, which blows my mind why you would ever hang up on somebody who's trying to sell you something that you might learn something about conversion rate and average invoice. You see, I had the Hoover vacuum person come to my house because I thrive by watching A players. A guy who sells a vacuum clearly could sell air conditioning. I'll tell you that. The person who is selling Dish Network was an amazing person making outbounds for me in my call center.

I'm always looking. My team is always looking for people who are alive and have a pulse. You see, if you're alive, have a pulse, and a half a smile, you think you could be happy, you may not be happy, but think you could be happy, then guess what? Bring it in. I tell people all the time. I don't need a diamond. You should wake up when you hear this everybody. I don't need a diamond. I need a piece of coal. I'll polish it. I'll polish it and I'll make it into the cleanest, best diamond you've ever seen. That's how I've been able to take the people that I have, I polish them, and polish them.

The other thing you need to be a company that's going to attract A players to your culture, you have to have core values. Now, I know a lot of companies they're like, oh, I got core values. I'm like, cool, throw it on me. They give me some crap-ass mission statement that they're reading off the wall. I'm like you don't even understand it. It's 30 years old. It doesn't even fit your culture today. You made it when it was you and your wife in the house trying to figure this all out. You know why they have the New Generation Coke, because the old generation Coke got old and sucked. That's why.

You have to look at that stuff. You need core values. What are the 4 core beliefs or 5 core beliefs? How many do you have? As many as make sense to your company, but as many as you can put in the DNA. Every one of our employees, how many? Every one of our employees know our core values. Our core values don't fit them just at gold medal service. They don't fit them just there. They fit them everywhere. They fit them in their own life because I learned that the closer I get them to understand that it's not life-business balance, its life-balance integration. It's not ... The core values we have in our company are no different than the core values they can live their personal life from.

Our number 2 core value, delivering wow service, exceeding customer's expectations, they could deliver wow service to their wife and their kids. Every day they should serve their wife and kids. Not okay, not the boring ass normal hugs you do, and I love you because you're like a walking dead, you're just on autopilot. I'm talking like how do you wow them? We make sure our core values build a culture that attracts people and builds a culture that allows us to integrate this into their life.

The last one part of this section I want to talk about is look, you're going to bring a guy you want to hire, A player, you want to put him in a 10-year-old truck with a hole in the floor. You got no branding that's attractable. It doesn't even look good. The tools are old. The material is beat up. It looks like a slob. There's maybe a bucket of piss in the back. Who's going to work for you? That sets the stage for your culture. Now, you don't need brand new sprinters, right. I bought 6 of them just last week. You don't need 6 new ones, but you can make an old vehicle look good and smell good. You could make it presentable where people will get it.

Very important, everything is important when you're recruiting. Most people treat recruiting, one thing's important. Get them in, run them through an interview process. That's not. See, it's the whole thing. I want you to treat recruiting like it's a mini business. It's a mini business or a second business to your business. That's how you have to treat it. The number 1 most important thing or I should say number 2, marketing is number 1. Recruiting is number 2. Recruiting is part of marketing.

Identify your culture. Does your culture attract what you want? Now, I'm going to give you something that's going to really sink this home.

You have to identify what you want. Oh, I'm looking for a plumber 10 years. No. No, you're not. That's not a great avatar. You see how cranked up you're getting? I can't even hear you and I'm getting cranked up. That's not a perfect avatar.

You want to know what is ... I'm looking for a 35-year-old guy with 5 years of plumbing experience that has young children, been married for 7 or 8 years, lives in this area. Loves to drive Corvette cars, rides a motorcycle on the weekend, loves to hang out on the beach and fish. I'm talking about you got to understand if you molded the perfect employee. I gave you a bucket full of clay and I said, "Build this and we'll jam a heart in it." That's what you got to identify.

You guys are just trying to get beating hearts that say they're A players. If you haven't figured out, most of your A players I bet were good people that were with you and they just did good in the beginning and grew with you. Most of them you hire that are like you would consider thoroughbreds, they never last long. They're always loose cannons, right. I believe sometimes it's better, most of the time to bring a B player, create them into an A than it ever is to find an A player. You have to identify what is the perfect avatar?

The second thing is where do they hang out? Where are they? If I'm in an area where NASCAR is big I'm looking for them at NASCAR. Hey, are you looking for a career change? Most people are just looking for the people there. How fast can you make a plumber into a plumber? I mean pretty darn fast. Okay, I get it, all of you guys that are plumbers on the call are like, "Ah, Mike, it's took me 25 years to become the pro and I could solve shit in my sleep." I get that. Can you get them to do 80%? How long does it take them to ... I'm no pro, but I changed the damn flapper. I've changed a toilet bowl and put a wax ring. Now there was no lead bend in it or anything. I don't know how to fix lead bends, some of you freaks out there now. Oh man, I go in there and I play with the lead bend. I get what you're saying.

I can get a guy who's mechanically inclined and turn them into doing water heaters and fixing copper pipes and solder it and spigot. Now I understand some of you guys got laws and regulations. I hear that all the time. "Oh, Mike, you don't have to licensing." Shit, if I had the licensing I'd build a licensing school. That's what I would do. Don't ever put a roadblock in front of my face because I will find 17 different ways to kick it and punch it down.

If I don't get, I will grab a sword, a gun, a cannon, a tank. Don't put a problem in front of me. I don't even understand problems. If it's a situation I'm going to kick it down. I'll build a school. You get my point that I'm saying here. Find where they're hanging your avatar. Are they at the gym? Are they in TM magazine? Are they in HVACR magazine? Where are they? Can I buy a list of them? We know the DNA. You guys know where the plumbers are hanging out. You know where the electricians hang out. You know the things they're reading.

Now I'm going to give you some marketing stuff soon, right. I'm going to start telling you about a plan. I'm going to touch base on a plan, on something that's really gonna help you guys with doable areas to go out there and make some magic. Okay, that's what I'm going to do. I'm going to go with that next. Let's just do another quick recap because I'm putting this into your brain for you, right?

We got to identify what is it we need before we need it. B players to make A players. Identify the culture, make sure it's like a magnet attracts, right. Identify the avatar. Do we know the exact makeup? When you can see that makeup now we can go out and talk to them. Now, before I go into the plan, this marketing plan and stuff, just because believe it or not we're 47 minutes in and I could do this for days and days. I do want to tell you guys, look, I do this to serve you. I want to tell you about my 4-day event. I'm not selling you nothing.

Some of you guys heard about it. Let me tell you a minute about it. I'm not selling you nothing. If it's a fit, you'll come. If it's not a fit love you guys anyway, I'm here to serve you. If you're interested and you think what I'm saying is game-changer stuff, I want you to imagine if you have seen it in real-time. I want you to imagine on day 1, I show you how to interview any from 20 to 50 people in one hour and how to facilitate this and the total process I go through. How to hire them that night and fill a room if you think that's magic, that alone you could see and go home and your investment would be free for itself.

I'm going to go into so many things just some I touch base on like core values and pre-rapport formula and how do you stack your inbound calls? How do you do 3 steps to close? I'll just tell you 1 more thing because most of you guys know me like look, the 4-day event you're going to spend 4 days with me. It would be like spending 4 days with Warren Buffet on steroids and physical fit and doing martial arts for 30 years, can break arrows and walk on fire, that's what 4 days is like. This isn't one of those things where we're tinkering around and we're done at 5. The first night we're done at 10:00 at night.

This is for warriors, okay, not for wimps. Day 2, by 6:00 you'll need a break from me. Day 3 we do dinner again, day 4 you're out by 5:00. You don't even leave the building until you have a roadmap to change your life and your business. You don't have a roadmap I don't go home. I have endurance. I could go for days and days and days. If any of that interests you, and I'll share our membership plans. We did 900,000 last year in memberships. We're going to do like $1.4 million probably in memberships only this year. If you want to know how I'm selling more 3-year memberships than 1-year memberships total and how my girl is selling over 125 of them a month on outbound calls. Her SPIF 2 months ago was $5100 in SPIF money that my $10 CSR made. If you want to learn that, that's what I do at my event. It's a no-brainer if you're looking to grow your company, twice, 3 times the size or gain your life back, come and spend 4 days with warriors and I'll show you some magic.

That's what I got for you. If you're interested you'll find a way to track me down either through Lyndsay, you'll email me at mikea@ceowarrior.com, you'll go through LinkedIn, you'll say you want it.

All right, let's go into the marketing stuff now. How do we actually go about, what are these other things? Well, 1st, look, recruiting never stops. You got to build a marketing recruiting world. That's what we gotta build, a recruiting world. I actually write a big globe. I make a big circle and I write all the areas. The 1st thing I say to myself is ... See, most people are trying just to attract the A player. See, I look and I create a relationship with A players. It's not about them just coming to me. It's about me serving them and them serving me in return.

I make sure, and a lot of companies don't have this, I make sure I have a very good package, a SPIF program, a bonus program, career opportunities for advancement. Anytime somebody comes into a culture and they see there's no room for advancement, where they think the top line is going to be there forever, you'll stop people from growing all the time. One of the best items, I'll tell you for recruiting, and benefits I'll share with you that we give our employees, we give them their birthday paid off. First off, just so you know, the number 1 most important person to any human being is their name.

Number 2 most important word today out there is free. Number 3, believe it or not, most important name is sex, so some of you guys just went to a dirty place so come back and stay with me on that. Giving somebody their birthday off is an amazing recruiting thing. Plus it's the little things that count. When you're recruiting having things like a food allowance, right, or a tool allowance, these are little things you can give that really show people that you care.

Now, the marketing recruiting strategies that you can implement today. One, you want to have a recruiting card. Okay, so we have a card that we share at the 4-day event, which actually is a nice card that I hired people, just so you know from Hooligan's, from Applebee's, everywhere. If you're in Dunkin Donuts we have a card that we'll hand and it's a recruiting card. It says, "Hey, if you're interested in an opportunity of a lifetime and being a winner give us a buzz. You've got nothing to lose. Come in, it's all confidential. If it's a fit, we'll talk, if it's not a fit, it's okay." That's 1 thing, the recruiting card.

Number 2, you want to have an incentive program built on your recruiting card. Your employees, if they recruit somebody, they come in, we hire them, after 90 days they get an incentive of some kind. It helps create a culture of they're going to be rewarded for that. The other thing is never waste time with one-on-one hiring. It's always a better facilitation if you interview multiple people at one time and it doesn't have to be the same position. We will interview electricians, plumbers, sales people, CSRs all in the same room at the same time.

It allows us to see the interaction between the people. Also, if you're doing one-on-one interviews for an hour my god 10 interviews is a long day, right. Who's got time for that? You don't need to do that. Next thing, direct mail. You can find a list of people that are subscribed to Plumber's magazine, TM magazine, or some kind of networking group. You can find a place where these people are, get a list, direct mail them, nice envelope, nice letterhead, throw a dollar inside or something and say, "Hey, here's a dollar for you to consider the opportunity of a lifetime. It's free to talk to me. It's completely ..." now, here's the magic that I want to tell you. "It's completely confidential." That's very important. Why? Look, if it's not a fit I don't want to feel at risk at all. Just like when you talk if you've ever been to the acquisition stage with people you would give them a letter of confidentiality, right, where you won't share that they're selling their business. You want to have that same thing for A players. A players, look, they don't want to be ... If it's not a fit you want to say okay and you want them to feel comfortable. You can use direct mail to reach out to these people.

Networking, so here's the thing about networking. You want to talk to all your vendors. Now don't post stuff in supply houses. It's just something for people to talk about you and graffiti it. What you want to always do is you want to have a separate email to every one of the supply houses or people, vendors you work with and you want to send them that you're offering an opportunity of a lifetime. Just so you know, I've hired, it was the regional manager of 7 or 8 Barnett stores. He worked in our Barnett, we have a Barnett inside our building that serves only us. We hired him.

I've hired my attorney that worked on a case for 2 years, he's with me 2 years, he works for me full-time now. Not because we have a lot of law stuff, he handles our warehouse, manages those and manages our accounting department. We're always out there letting people know what we're looking for and we're very clear in sharing the avatar we're looking for.

Now, some of these avenues may not fit you guys because maybe you're not at the size or you are, but billboard is a recruiting strategy. TV is a recruiting strategy. Radio is a recruiting strategy. Acquisition, we send out an acquisition letter. Now just so you guys know I've never acquired 1 company. I got the 23.5 million, I never acquired. Not that I'm against acquiring, because most people today think their business is worth too much. If it's not a perfect lineup acquisition they don't have good employees that are going to fit me. They don't have good products they've been selling. Their customers they're not the premier customers the way we serve them, well, then I'm not going to spend money. If I take that same money and throw it into marketing I could get better results because I know my avatar for marketing.

Acquisition, if you send out an acquisition letter you might have somebody interested that's tired that's looking for an amazing opportunity, you could bring them aboard. Here's one most people forget about. I was just reminded the other day, old employee networks. Everybody that works for you in the past that might have been good and moved on or someone 10 years ago that wasn't good may be great today.

I just got back a salesman just came back to me. He was gone for 3 years. 3 years ago he sold $3,000,000 plus he made $275,000 plus working for me. I don't know why he went on. Things, life changed, he moved on. We kept in touch with him always and now he decided to come back. His first day back he's selling sewers and he sold $20,000 worth of sewers yesterday. Stay in touch with your old networks. As much as employees should never burn the bridge, owners should never burn the bridge either. Make sure you leave the gateway open because other people's opportunities might lose and they might want to come back to you.

The other thing is mystery shopping is a great strategy for getting people in your house if you want to mystery shop other companies. Now look, I'm okay mystery shopping companies. I'm going to tell you why. Nobody leaves a company they love. I mystery shop like god knows how many times people are mystery. I've been, people tried to recruit me, they've grabbed my employees list.

I'll tell you a story. One time a roto-rooter grabbed my employees list and the recruiter they tried offering all my guys $50 an hour. I just flipped it around in my company and said, "Hey, get me every business card you get me from a roto-rooter company I'll give you 25 bucks." They were cutting off people on the highways and getting business cards from people. At the end of the day when your culture is a culture of warriors and a pack of wolves it's hard to steal. You can't do it. Mystery shopping is an opportunity for some of you guys.

Social media. I love it when people are telling me, "I need people. I need people." I'm like, "Cool. I was on your Facebook. I've never seen you post a damn recruiting ad with a great opportunity. I've never seen you on LinkedIn. I've never seen you in the plumbing LinkedIn groups telling people you have an amazing opportunity. I've never even seen you do this shit. I've never seen you run Facebook ads for recruiting to people that have plumbing in their thing. How bad do you need somebody or are you just lying to me again?"

You have this whole social media avenue. How much social media do you do? You do as much as you need to get people. As much as you need to get people. Now when I said to mystery shop I want to let you know about competitors. I'm a great player in the market with competitors. I support the competitors. I don't badmouth the competitors unless they try to hurt me. I've been trying to be hurt a lot, otherwise I support. I want all competitors to do great because there's so much business out there and there's so many employees.

There's recruiting companies you can work with. You can make a deal with a recruiting company that you'll only pay if they find someone and hire them for 90 days. Military, I love military people. Let me just tell you about military people. First off, I'm glad they're in the world today because they keep me alive and allow me to have the business and life I have. That's why I put up that big ass flag in the front of my building was because I have 20% of my employees are military. They're smart. I don't have to tell them to show up on time. They always look good. We just hired another one. He worked on jets. He retired from the Air Force working on jets.

How hard do you think it's going to be for me to get him to work on electrical panel on an HVAC unit? He fixed damn jets. I'm pretty sure he can fix a furnace or an air conditioner. All the military stations we're constantly telling them when guys retire from military we know that one of the biggest struggles is to figure out what's next, right, to have another mission. Gold Medal is a great mission for them, so there's another great avenue.

We have trade source companies. Now sometimes you just need people now, but you don't need them, you get big jobs in or some guys have commercial work and stuff and there's different trade source companies where you can hire employees, hire them for a day. I've also learned that there's a lot of these places that are mechanics, right, and it's funny some people have become mechanics and go to school for it and they love it. Some they hate it once they're doing it for a little while and mechanics make amazing trades people because they're mechanically inclined. They know how to not break nuts and bolts and stuff. Mechanic areas.

Trade schools are incredible. Now again I'll tell you some areas don't have trade schools. Start a damn trade school. If you can't find one near you, build one. That's what I believe. How hard is it to get a trade school? You could do it one night a week, but trade schools Lincoln Tech, all these type of places around the world, you become friends with them and let them know we always have opportunities.

Now, when we do our special what I call hiring experience, it's a different than a job fair. A hiring experience is like we're totally engaged. It is the funniest thing, it's like a rock band, fun type stuff you come to. We tell the trade schools every time we're having those. They send people to us.

Let me give you one of the biggest things we do. We're constantly, oh, I got another nugget actually I just thought of. This is, holy shit, I better type this before it loses. Hang on guys, you have to wait so I don't lose this out of my brain here.

Okay, whew, I didn't want to even lose that one. All right. The thing about trade schools and stuff when you talk to them is don't just look for who's graduating today. Like I told someone the other day I'm like, "You went trade schools?" They're like, "Yeah, you know, the graduate ..." I'm like, "How long has the trade school been around?" They're like, "50 years." I'm like, "Okay, where's the people that were in it 10 years ago?" You have to sometimes ask the right questions. Don't assume people will have the strategy for you.

Same thing you might have had junior techs that worked for you or apprentices 10 years ago and they're probably full-blown plumbers right now. I have an electrician that worked for me holy crap it's got to be 17, 18 years ago and he's not in the service business he went into the industrial business and he's been in it for 18 years now or something or 15 years. He's a cracker jack electrician industrial and commercial. If I did that I'd try to recruit him, but he doesn't want to do what I do.

Look, it's very few people are going to stay bad forever. Your past employees and your past apprentices, schools that had people 5 and 10 years ago, are all possible great people today. Remember when you start looking more for B players and create a culture and facilitate an environment of taking B players to A players, from C to B and B to A, you'll create a culture of this improvement.

Now I've also learned, I'll give a little tip, I wasn't thinking of this one, but I'll give it because it came to my brain. We create what we call a mentor program. We have team members in our company, they're not field supervisors, they can't find people, they can't tell them they suck or anything, their whole job is just to take an A player that we have, to take a B player underneath his wing. A lot of people tell me, "Well, what do you give them for that?" I give them nothing for that. I give them the satisfaction. I'm a culture of serving, just like you guys told me how valuable some of this stuff was. Holy crap you feel the beef. You turned me into a hulk. I'm like boom, what's the next tele-seminar I'm going to do and serve to you guys?

A mentor program is that person can take them under their wing, because I believe there's no soldiers left behind. My culture does not allow anybody to under-perform because my culture will not let somebody else not serve themselves, their wives, or their children. We won't do that. We will do everything legal, and shit if it was 20 years ago I'd kick their ass to do it. Some men just need to be kicked in the face and chopped in the throat so that they can serve at the highest level.

The mentor does it. He can, in the truck, say things that I couldn't say. I can't tell him to say that, but he can say, "Dude, get your head out of your ass already. What the heck's broken here, man? How are you serving customers?" Your report card is the value of revenue another human will give you and say thank you today. If you don't receive revenue from a customer, they don't pay you well and pay you for extra jobs you delivered a shitty service. That's your confirmation of the level of service you deliver.

The mentor, team mentor program is about that person taking somebody on their wing and not sleeping until they help him. Why don't I pay them extra for that? Look, you can't really ever take a great tech and make him a great manager. You can take a great amazing tech and you can turn him into a field mentor. You could turn him into a team leader and train him on leaderships and skill sets and training and coaching and then you can move him. Then you can move him to be a manager. You can't take a tech to being a manager because he doesn't have the skillset. I watched that, I made that mistake a long time ago myself. I made that mistake.

Let's do a summary of this whole thing about this recruiting. 1, I want you, in your mind right now, we'll do this exercise from 1 to 10. Everybody, you're on here because you need people. 1 to 10, 10 is I know I need somebody and 10 is I've been giving it so much effort. I have not walked by a human being in a store anywhere and not told them I have an opportunity, and 1, you're not doing it really well. Give yourself a number from 1 to 10. 10 your recruiting has been a priority. You've worked it night and day. You've been on the phone. You've called old employees. You are so exhausting it and 1 you're not doing it at all.

I'll tell you most people are doing it a 5. Anytime you do something at 50% you're going to get 50% results or worse, right? You have to make it 100%. I just thought of something else I wanted to tell you guys. This is amazing. You'll love this one. Here is a magic question.

Magic question, everybody you do an interview with or everybody who comes in front of you, you want to ask this: Hey, if you did know another plumber, electrician, HVAC tech, drain cleaning tech, okay, CSR, salesman, that was amazing that you ever worked with anywhere in your past career, who would that be and when was it? That is the magic question.

Who would that be and when was it? They're going to say, "Man, I worked with a guy, Jack, he was off the hook. He was like the number 1" "Jack who?" He'll say, "Jack, the name, right," I'll be like, "Oh, where was he from?" Once I have a name, I'm in Facebook, I'm in LinkedIn, I'm finding this dude. Hey man, "Do you have a cell number for Jack? Do you keep in touch with him?" "I do." "Would you give him a call right now and tell him we might have an opportunity?" I'll say, "It looks very great for you, too." If I got to have you and Jack it's great. Every person who comes in who's not a fit they know 2 or 3 people that are a fit. I mean who the hell doesn't know a plumber today or an electrician?

When you ask people especially if they've been in the career for 5 or 10 years you gotta bet they've met and known people out there. You just have to understand the question to ask. Then that will help you recruit.

This report comes with a couple of special bonuses...

Audio Replay of the Live Event
http://events.instantteleseminar.com/?eventid=69622779

Bonus Truth About Hiring Video
https://ceowarrior.com/truth-about-hiring

Wait! You're not done yet. If you put this report on the shelf now, you'll risk completely wasting the strategies and ideas you just read. Turn them into action right away. On the next page you can start turning my ideas into your business-building action. Fill it out right now...

TAKE ACTION

Want to extract all the value you can from this report? Don't just put this book on the shelf. Review this report and fill out the list below, writing out the actions you should stop doing, keep doing, and start doing. On the next page is space to make additional notes. And for further actions, be sure to continue reading the bonus report and added strategies and resources on the following pages!

Stop Doing (Actions you're doing now but need to stop doing)

_____

_____

_____

_____

Keep Doing (Actions you're doing now and should continue)

_____

_____

_____

_____

Start Doing (Actions you're not doing now but should start)

_____

_____

_____

_____

Additional Notes

SPECIAL REPORT: NETWORKING YOUR WAY TO BROKE

HERE'S HOW SERVICE BUSINESS OWNERS FIND THE ONE INDUSTRY GROUP THAT WILL ACTUALLY MAKE A MEASURABLE DIFFERENCE TO THEIR BUSINESS' GROWTH... INSTEAD OF THROWING MONEY AWAY AT HIGH-COST, LOW-VALUE MEMBERSHIPS

This report is for service business owners – including plumbers, HVAC, and electricians – who understand the importance that an industry organization or group can play in the growth of their business.

If you are either currently looking for an industry organization or group to join or are disappointed by the results you're (not) getting from the organization you currently belong to, then make sure you read this report all the way through because you may be surprised by what you learn...

You're on a journey and you reach a fork in the road. But not just two potential paths... Rather, you have a dozen or more potential paths. Each path promises to help you get to your preferred destination but when you look at the dejected faces of people traveling in the opposite direction, you know that not every path will do what it promises.

Welcome to the world of home service industry organizations and groups. There are many available and each one promises to train you to grow your service business with the latest strategies and industry best practices, to provide networking opportunities, and perhaps discounts on marketing or services.

Unfortunately, many service business owners learn the hard way that these organizations are not delivering on their promise; instead, they

happily accept your hard-earned money for their expensive memberships but rarely deliver back the value you hope to get.

Year after year you promise yourself, this year I'll dig deeper to get more out of the group, or, this year I'll try a different group; but you get to the end of every year and discover that nothing has changed. Your money has been wasted. (And yet, if you're like most service business owners, you continue in the organization because you hope that next year will bring you the value you need.")

The results speak for themselves: you might take away a half-decent idea now and then, or you might benefit from the occasional group call… but you have a hard time justifying the membership cost.

Forget the empty promises of training and networking that will once again fall through.

What do service business owners really want? If you're like most service business owners out there, you probably want **practical ideas that you can implement immediately to get fast results; and, to be frank, you might even benefit from the occasional get-your-ass-in-gear push to help you overcome the frustrations and obstacles that plague you daily.**

Use this list to diagnose whether you're wasting your money at your current industry organization or group, and to see what option will actually create positive measurable growth in your business.

#1. Are The Owners "In The Trenches" Every Day?

Some industry organizations and groups are run by people who haven't run a home service business in years; others are run by people who have never worked a single day in the home service industry!

CEO Warrior is owned by Mike Agugliaro and Rob Zadotti, who also own Gold Medal Service. Gold Medal Service is New Jersey's #1 home service business, employing 190 staff, serving 125,000 customers, and will earn more than $30 million this year. Mike and Rob still run their home service business and are always learning and testing to share only the strategies that have proven to work.

Would you rather hear from someone who is no longer in the business or someone who is still in the business daily?

#2. Have The Owners Of Your Industry Organization Discovered The Path To Success?

Many industry organizations simply pass down their best practices from one generation to the next, and those who run the organization just "parrot" what they've heard before. If they're in the industry, they're just moderately successful... or perhaps have merely inherited their thriving home service business rather than built it up from scratch.

Mike and Rob started out as electricians. For the first decade of their business the two of them worked 24/7 and struggled to make ends meet. After nearly burning out and shutting the business down they decided to fix what was broken, so they invested heavily in their own education then rebuilt the business from the ground up. The next eleven years were completely different, with year-over-year growth of more than a million dollars annually.

Would you rather get "hearsay advice" that is parroted from a previously successful person, or learn the strategies and systems from the same person who struggled then figured it out?

#3. Do the Owners Invest Heavily In Education?

If you currently belong to an industry organization or group, find out what the owners have learned recently. Ask them. Do they have a growing knowledgebase of current field-tested strategies that they've culled from the best-of-the-best?

CEO Warrior does! Mike and Rob have invested more than $900,000 into their education and have studied the best strategies even from organizations outside of the home service industry. Disney, Zappos, Amazon,

Nordstrom, Joe Polish, and others – CEO Warrior mines the best strategies from these best-of-the-best companies.

Do you prefer stale strategies that have not been updated in years or the latest field-tested ideas inspired by the world's best-of-breed companies?

#4. Does The Industry Organization Have A Million Dollar Guarantee?

When you attend an industry event, what kind of guarantee do they have? Many don't offer any kind of guarantee; at best, you might hear the vague "If you're not satisfied, we'll try to make it right" promise.

CEO Warrior's 4-day Warrior Fast Track Academy events come with an iron-clad $1 million dollar guarantee that promises: **"If you get to the end of the very first day and you haven't learned enough strategies that will make you an extra million dollars or save you a million dollars, then simply ask for a refund and you'll get 100% of your tuition, PLUS the cost of airfare and hotel to get to the event, on the spot... no questions asked."**

What's the guarantee of the industry event you attend?

#5. Does The Industry Organization Provide Swipe-And-Deploy Marketing Templates?

Many home service business owners fiercely protect their marketing and will never share it. That same thinking is carried over into industry organizations where you might (but probably won't) get "plain vanilla" marketing ideas that may or may not work.

CEO Warrior is different, though. You get a binder that is literally stuffed with marketing templates that are actually being used right now in the marketplace, bringing in millions of dollars of business monthly for Gold Medal Service. When you receive these marketing templates at a 4-day Warrior Fast Track Academy event, you have permission to modify and use them in your own business – and you'll even be introduced to the name of the printer who can print them for you!

In your current industry group, were you handed a big swipe file and introduced to the exact people who were able to deploy it for you?

#6. Does The Industry Organization Feel Like A Brotherhood?

When you attend an industry event at your organization, what does it feel like? Do you nod silently to the other attendees before stealing a quick glance at their name tag because you can't remember who they are? You barely remember anyone's names because you just don't engage with these people enough.

At CEO Warrior, you may join the CEO Warrior Circle, which is a tight-knit brotherhood of service business owners. You'll be on a first-name basis and think of these other men and women as more than just colleagues – but as friends, family, and fellow "Warriors" as you fight together to grow your service businesses. CEO Warrior Circle members become a family and will do ANYTHING for each other, supporting each other professionally and personally.

When was the last time you felt like you were part of a close-knit brotherhood that cared about your success?

#7. Are You Just Paying For Friendships?

In most organizations, you're paying that expensive membership fee for what – a few friendships that you might or might not value outside of the networking event?

At CEO Warrior, you'll make solid friendships with other CEO Warrior Circle members but the real value of the group is the life-changing results that can transform your business and deliver more wealth, freedom, and market domination. You'll be connected to a strong group of fellow Warriors, each of whom is highly interested in your success. You'll make friends, yes, but you'll discover that the CEO Warrior Circle is all about helping you grow your business to create the business and life that you want.

Wouldn't you rather invest in yourself and your business than for expensive friendships?

#8. Do The Large Companies Just Promote Themselves?

In many industry organizations and groups, you'll encounter business owners of all sizes… And usually the small guys will chase around the big guys and try to find out what their secrets are (only to have the big guys simply promote themselves without ever sharing good ideas.)

CEO Warrior Circle is not about self-promotion but about everyone pulling together so that everyone can win. Each Warrior steps up and is willing to help the others. **What kind of brotherhood is CEO Warrior Circle? You could probably call any of them in the middle of the night for an emergency and they'd be there for you. Could you do that in your current industry organization or group?**

Would you rather hear a big company talk about themselves or a successful company share their best ideas with you?

#9. How Long Do You Have To Wait To Get Support?

One frustration that you may have with your industry organization is how long you have to wait to hear back from someone, especially if you're looking for help or advice. Maybe they only respond during business hours, or maybe they promise a 48 hour window to reply.

Mike and the CEO Warrior team are very responsive – **offering insight and advice in social posts, live video, email, and text messages at just about any time of day or night.** They recognize how important the Warriors are and they strive to serve them.

Would you rather wait hours (or days) to get help, or get help right away?

#10. Does Your Organization Take A One-Size-Fits-All Approach?

Nothing is more frustrating than getting some useful-sounding strategies… only to discover that these strategies only work in a business that is different than yours. Maybe you run a rural business but the ideas only work in town; maybe you have a team of 5 but the ideas only work if you have a team of 100.

CEO Warrior serves businesses of all sizes, in all locations. No matter how your business is configured, the strategies and guidance you'll receive will be custom-tailored to fit YOUR unique situation. There are Warriors all over the world – every size of business in many different markets. The strategies you get will work in your situation. Period.

Would you rather hear general advice that might not apply to you or the best field-tested strategies that will work in your specific situation?

#11. Is There An Emphasis On Growing Your Business Or Growing Your Life?

The last time you were at an organization or group event, how much emphasis was placed on your life? Probably very little. Most industry organizations try to help you grow your business – that's their purpose. Problem is, they don't care where you get the time and energy to make the necessary changes.

At CEO Warrior, the emphasis is on growing your business so that you can have the life you want. You'll learn the strategies to grow your business and you'll also discover how a healthy family life can help your business (and vice versa). You'll even hear how to stay healthy through the life and lifestyle of a service business owner.

Why grow your business at the expense of your family when you can have both – a successful business and a fulfilling family life?

#12. Does Your Group Tell You The Honest Truth, Even If It Hurts?

Most of us want to hear nice things – but if you're reading this then you're smart enough to know that a hurtful truth is better than a comforting lie. Yet, how often does your industry organization or group say something harsh but necessary? (Hint: they probably won't because they want you to renew your membership!)

Mike Agugliaro is known for his no holds barred, no BS approach. If a Warrior needs to hear something, Mike will say it. The honest truth, even if occasionally hurtful, is far more advantageous to hear. And, it's not just an honest truth told to you, there's also ongoing accountability to "hold your feet to the fire" to help you do what you say you're going to do.

If you'd rather be lied to, then join some other group. But wouldn't you rather hear the truth if it benefits you?

#13. Does Your Group "Nickel-And-Dime" You For Different Services?

In a lot of industry groups and organizations, members pay a membership fee to get access to a few things, and then they're expected to pay extra for additional products and services (like events and extra coaching).

CEO Warrior Circle members enjoy an all-inclusive experience where unlimited coaching, events, and resources are included as part of the membership investment. You simply won't get another bill for needing extra help.

Does your current group or organization care more about the fee or about you?

#14. Do You Get To Learn Directly From The Guru, Or Are You Pushed Off To Some Trainer-For-Hire?

Maybe this has happened to you: you pay your membership fee and you look forward to hearing from the guru or main person behind the group… until you actually start to interact with the group and you find out that you're stuck with a trainer-for-hire working out of a call center who follows a script and references the same resources you received when you first joined.

CEO Warrior Circle members get full access to Mike and Rob and the Master Coach Trainers – an elite group of experts who are in the industry daily. Whether by phone, text, or email (as well as webinars and events), you'll interact with the same gurus who start CEO Warrior Circle.

When was the last time you heard from the guru in your group?

#15. Do You Learn Cutting Edge Internet Marketing Strategies?

A lot of groups teach generic marketing strategies with little, if any, internet marketing. And many groups that do teach internet marketing are teaching things that worked for them 5, 10, and even 15 years ago.

CEO Warrior Circle members get the latest cutting edge internet marketing strategies that work right now for service businesses – and the reason these work is because they're being constantly tested and refined.

How current are the internet strategies you've learned? (Have you learned any? Are they currently being used?)

#16. Do They Share A Lot Of Information For Free?

Most industry groups will make a lot of promises about what you'll get when you join and force you to pay thousands of dollars to actually access the information. Very few will even give you a little glimpse into what you can learn, forcing you to put up a lot of money to find see if they're for real.

At CEO Warrior, you can learn so many strategies – whether by books, social media (Facebook, LinkedIn, and Twitter), or CEOWARRIOR.com, Mike shares many of his best ideas and strategies. In fact, one person watched Mike's free videos and applies his strategies over a 2-year period and increased the number of techs in his business from six to 20. And, many more business owners see even bigger results faster by attending Mike's 4-day Warrior Fast Track Academy

Could you more-than-triple your workforce from the free information provided by your industry group?

#17. Do You Get A Free 30 Minute Strategy Session To Even See If This Is The Right Fit For You?

Most industry organizations and groups will tell you to pay if you want to find out whether it's right for you or not. You risk your money and time without really knowing until it's too late whether the information you're learn is helpful. Perhaps they throw some generic ideas at you in an attempt to wow you but they're just regurgitating the same information for everyone.

At CEO Warrior, no one can attend the Warrior Fast Track Academy without first getting a free 30 minute strategy session with Mike, Rob, or a Master Coach Trainer. These strategy sessions are FOR you and ABOUT the strategy, problem, question, challenge, or opportunity of YOUR choosing. Simply share the struggle you want help with and the Master Coach Trainer will work with you – for free – before you can even attend the Warrior Fast Track Academy.

When was the last time you got a 30 minute free personal one-on-one strategy session with your industry organization before they even allowed you to move forward with them?

#18. Are There Events That Your Family Wants To Attend (That Actually Help Your Family Members Understand What You Do?)

Most industry events are technical and boring. Your family begs not to go, and they don't really care what you learn while you're there. But wouldn't it be nice if they could attend to understand what you do? And wouldn't it be amazing if they had such a good time that they begged to go back again? CEO Warrior Circle members often bring their spouses to events – from regular Circle events to special Warrior Relationship events, your spouse will love the event and will have a better understanding of what you do so they can support you as you grow your business.

When was the last time you attended an event with your spouse… and your spouse asked to go back again?

#19. Do You Dread Those BORING Live Events?

Most industry events are a bore! Look around the room and you'll see people trying to stay awake while the speaker drones on and on. You keep checking your watch. You drain your coffee cup and can't wait for a break to refill it. You spend more time checking your phone for messages than you do watching another boring PowerPoint slide presentation.

CEO Warrior events, including the Warrior Fast Track Academy, are anything but boring. Audiences are captivated by Mike's style, by his strategies, and by his level of service that he brings to every presentation. Some CEO Warrior Circle events even include firewalking! Make sure you get a good night's sleep before the event because you'll be "on" the entire time, and you'll leave with a level of inspiration and energy you didn't think was possible!

When was the last time you actually were excited about attending an industry event?

#20. Do You Leave The Live Event With A Road Map Of Success?

Many people attend industry events with the hope of getting a couple of good ideas that they can bring back to their company (and sometimes they'll even remember to implement those ideas when they get back!)

But those who attend Mike Agugliaro's Warrior Fast Track Academy events get something different: you'll work WITH Mike throughout the 4-day event to create your own customized 90 Day Road Map that outlines the step-by-step strategies you want to implement in your business to grow in the next 90 days. And by the end of the event, Mike and his team will even check your Road Map to make sure it's clear and achievable so you can start implementing it immediately. (Some attendees even start implementing before they leave the event.)

When was the last time you left an industry event with a multi-million dollar step-by-step Road Map to implement in the next 90 days?

The choice is yours – will you continue paying for an industry group or organization that…

… doesn't deliver what it promises?
… takes your money and then asks for more?
… feels like an expensive way to meet a few other friends in the industry?
… is difficult to reach anybody when you need real help?
… doesn't share the best, most effective field-tested strategies and ideas?
… run by people who aren't in the industry?
… doesn't seem to care about your business (or your family)?

Or, will you finally step and realize that YOU and YOUR BUSINESS (and YOUR FAMILY) are worth making the switch to a group like CEO Warrior – a true brotherhood of like-minded business owners who want help each other, led by an industry leader who will always be there for you?

The very first step to learn more about how CEO Warrior is different is to attend the 4-day Warrior Fast Track Academy – to learn more, to get many of the benefits described above, and to see if the CEO Warrior Circle is right for you.

Go to <u>WarriorFastTrackAcademy.com</u> to apply.

Are you tired of treading water – staying busy in your business but never really getting ahead? **Are you ready to discover the most powerful strategies to create real change, growth, and market domination in your business?**

Whether you're new and totally overwhelmed or you're a seasoned pro and looking for to reignite, The **Warrior Fast Track Academy** can show you how to get to the next level.

Warrior Fast Track Academy is my 4-day hands-on event where I guide you and a group of like-minded service business owners through the exact plan that I used to build a $30+ million (and growing) business. I'll reveal the blueprint and show you how you can implement the same blueprint into your business, with all areas of mastery planned out and ready to be plugged in. You'll be motivated and inspired to lead positive, profitable change in your company and take your business to never-before-seen heights.

Business owners who have attended the Warrior Fast Track Academy have said it's "life changing" and gone on to build successful businesses all around the world.

If you want to take control of your business and your future, Warrior Fast Track Academy is THE event to make that happen. To see what others are saying about Warrior Fast Track Academy, to learn more about my $1 million guarantee, and to pre-register for an upcoming event, go to **WarriorFastTrackAcademy.com**

"You are the average of the 5 people you spend the most time with."
(Jim Rohn)

... Who are YOU spending time with?

Here's the fastest way to leverage the power of proximity by spending time with like-minded action-takers who work together – to grow your business while striving to become unstoppable.

Most industry groups and organizations take your money and give you just a few stale best practices and networking opportunities. But at CEO Warrior, we've created **a powerful, exclusive "family of Warriors" who discover the best secrets and field-tested strategies, and who hold each other accountable while implementing them.**

Welcome to the **exclusive, invitation-only CEO Warrior Circle** where business owners can join to become Warriors and inspiring leaders of a strong and growing business.

During the upcoming year, we'll revolutionize your business and your life. We'll blow your wealth, freedom and personal goals out of the water by focusing on massive business building and life strategies. From weekly calls to exclusive events, from one-on-one coaching to an exclusive vault of swipe-and-deploy resources, joining the CEO Warrior Circle gives you everything you need to grow your business.

This program is designed for action-takers who are ready to make the commitment and take action to boost their business.

To learn more about the Warrior Circle, and to see if you qualify to participate in the Mastermind, get in touch at CEOWARRIOR.com/contact

READ THE FREE MAGAZINE WRITTEN FOR THE HOME SERVICE INDUSTRY

Discover new information, insight, and industry-specific success stories in Home ServiceMAX – the free online magazine written for home service business owners.

Each issue of Home ServiceMAX is packed with practical tips and strategies that you can implement right away into your home service business. They're field-tested and written by experts and industry insiders.

Home ServiceMAX will help you improve your sales, marketing, finance, human resources and customer service. Keep it on hand as you develop best practices to meet your team's unique challenges.

Whether you're a plumber, electrician, carpenter, roofer, builder, painter or specialist in any other service industry trade, to survive you must also stand out as a business leader. We designed this magazine to help you achieve that goal.

Each easy-to-read issue is available online for free. Check out the articles and make sure you have a pen and paper in hand to write down all the actions you'll want to take when you're done each article.

Read the current issue and subscribe here: HomeServiceMaxMag.com

ABOUT THE AUTHOR

Mike Agugliaro, Business Warrior

As Seen On

Mike Agugliaro helps his clients grow their service businesses utilizing his $30 Million Warrior Fast Track Academy Blueprint, which teaches them how to achieve massive wealth and market domination.

Two decades ago he founded Gold Medal Electric with his business partner Rob. After nearly burning out, he and Rob made a change: they developed a powerful blueprint that grew the company. Today, Gold Medal Service is now the top service industry provider in Central New Jersey. With over 190 staff and 140+ trucks on the road, Gold Medal Service now earns over $30 million in revenue each year.

Mike is a transformer who helps service business owners and other entrepreneurs master themselves and their businesses, take control of their dreams and choices, and accelerate their life and business growth to new heights. Mike is the author of the popular book The Secrets Of Business Mastery, in which he reveals 12 areas that all service business owners need to master.

Mike speaks and transforms around the world; his Warrior Fast Track Academy events are popular, transformational events for service business owners; he also leads a mastermind of business owners known as Warrior Circle. Mike has been featured in MSNBC, Financial Times, MoneyShow, CEO World, and more.

Mike is an avid martial artist who has studied karate, weaponry, jujitsu, and has even developed his own martial art and teaches it to others. The discipline of martial arts equips him to see and act on opportunities, create change in himself and others, and see that change through to successful completion.

Mike is a licensed electrician and electrical inspector, he is a certified Master Fire Walk Instructor, certified professional speaker, and a licensed practitioner of Neuro-Linguistic Programming (NLP).

Whether firewalking, breaking arrows on his neck, studying martial arts, transforming businesses, or running his own business, Mike Agugliaro leads by powerful example and is changing the lives and businesses of service business owners everywhere.

Mike lives in New Jersey with his wife and two children.

IN THE MEDIA

An article published in the HVACR Business Magazine discussing the struggles of being a service business owner and sharing his Situation Analysis Tool to help make better business decisions.

READ

ceowarrior.com/hvacr

Featured in a TV segment on the Nightly Business Report on CNBC. This interview shares how Mike, as an electrician, started his own business and is now advising other entrepreneurs how to be a CEO Warrior in their business.

WATCH

ceowarrior.com/cnbc

This article is about strategies to build a strong and productive team. This is one of many articles that Mike has published through Comfortech.

READ

ceowarrior.com/contractor

Mike shares 5 powerful mindset shifts to rapidly grow your business. These are some that helped him grow his $28M business.

READ

ceowarrior.com/ceoworld

IN THE MEDIA

Mike shares tips on how to motivate your staff by discovering their why. It's a strategy he uses to leverage and motivate his staff of 190 with great success.

READ

ceowarrior.com/thenews

Vendors are a great resource – and Mike explains why. He explains how you should choose your vendors to create stronger and more lucrative relationships and partnerships. This article was also published in Entrepreneur!

ceowarrior.com/foxnews

MSNBC interviews Mike Agugliaro and business partner Rob Zadotti to share how they grew their service business from $1M a year to over $28M one employee at a time, through processes and systems.

READ

ceowarrior.com/msnbc

CEO Warrior Owner Mike Agugliaro Hosts Fast Track CEO Workshop, Sept. 13-16

CBS8 featured an article about Mike, CEO Warrior and the 4 Day Warrior Fast Track Academy and how it helps service business owners.

READ

ceowarrior.com/cbs8

The Secrets Of Business Mastery: Build Wealth, Freedom and Market Domination For Your Service Business in 12 Months or Less*. A chapter-by-chapter collection of best business practices, tools and strategies for service business owners.

Secrets of Leadership Mastery: 22 Powerful Keys To Unlock Your Team's Potential and Get Better Result*s: 22 powerful keys to help you create a culture where you build and lead a hardworking team of superstars, inspire them to give their very best, and generate measurable results.

Secrets of Communication Mastery: 18 Laser Focused Tactics To Communicate More Effectively*. We all communicate. We can all learn to communicate more effectively. When you do, you'll see instant results in every personal and professional relationship.

Timeless Secrets of A Warrior*. Discover the most powerful, time-tested Warrior secrets that will propel you toward success by revealing strategies from some of history's greatest minds.

9 Pillars Of Business Mastery Program*: Discover the nine most powerful and transformative strategies that are PROVEN to completely transform your business and your life.

CONNECT WITH MIKE AGUGLIARO

Connect with Mike in the following places and find even more free resources and strategies to help you grow your business.

Website: CEOWARRIOR.com – Go here now to get free resources, including chapters from Mike's book and a library of resources.

Warrior App: CEOWARRIOR.com/warriorapp – stay up-to-date on the latest strategies and events by downloading the Warrior App for iOS and Android.

Podcast: CEOWARRIOR.com/podcast

Events: CEOWARRIOR.com/events

Social: Visit CEOWARRIOR.com to connect with Mike on Facebook, Twitter, LinkedIn, and elsewhere.

Home ServiceMAX Magazine: HomeServiceMaxMag.com